Ena,
BE
COURAGEOUS!!

Your LO '88
classmate

10/2014

FEELING Tall

Eight SHORT lessons on courage and change

JEFF WILLIAMSON

Sycamore Tree Communications • Knoxville, TN

No part of this publication may be reproduced in whole or in part, or stored in a retrieval system, or transmitted in any form or by any means, electronic, mechanical, photocopying, recording, or otherwise, without written permission of the publisher. For information regarding permission, write to Sycamore Tree Communications, 9725 Stone Henge Lane, Knoxville, TN, 37922.

Copyright © 2003 Sycamore Tree Communications

ISBN 0-9721366-0-6

All rights reserved.
Sycamore Tree Communications
9725 Stone Henge Lane, Knoxville, TN, 37922

Cover and interior design © TLC Graphics, www.TLCGraphics.com.

Printed in U.S.A.
First printing, June 2003

Dedication

To my son Matthew, whose intelligence keeps me on my toes.

To my daughter Ciara, whose grace keeps me humble.

To my youngest, Candace, whose energy keeps me young.

And to my girlfriend and wife, Meryl, who has followed me through every turn we have taken as a family.

With all my heart I dedicate this book to you.

Acknowledgments

I could do nothing in my life without God, whom I thank with all my heart, soul, and mind. The gospel singer Andre Crouch phrased it best when he said, "The voices of a million angels could not express my gratitude, all that I am and ever hope to be, I owe it all to thee."

Much love to my father and mother, Mr. And Mrs. Henry and Willie Lee Williamson. They did their best to raise five boys, and if I'm doing the grading, I give them an A.

Thanks also to my brothers, who encouraged me through the process. Eric, David, Gerald, and Antweyne, you guys are all right.

To my editors — Dr. Pearl Bell, Robyn Wheeler, Martin Haire, Peter Vogt, Lewis Moyse, my wife Meryl, and principal editor Leslie LaChance — thanks so much for your contributions.

To Tami Dever and Erin Stark at TLC Graphics, the professionals who walked me through this process and I love you for it.

Table of Contents

Introduction ix

Chapter One 1
Others May Look Down on You,
But Never Look Down on Yourself

Chapter Two 13
Underestimate Me ... Please!

Chapter Three 21
Sometimes a Whippin' Is a Good Thing

Chapter Four 29
Face the Facts and Move Forward

Chapter Five 37
Be Tough, but Nice

Chapter Six 43
Get Ahead of the Crowd

Chapter Seven 51
Paint Your Picture for the World

Chapter Eight 59
Don't Let the Tall People Have All the Fun

Introduction

William James, the 19th century historian, once wrote:
> "Whenever two people meet, there are really six present. There is each man as he sees himself, each as the other person sees him, and each man as he really is."

What others think of you may not be the you that you really are.

As a kid, I really had a complex about my height. A little guy then and measuring a whopping 5 feet 4 inches now, I thought height was all people saw when they were in my presence. But as I got a little older, I learned a lot about those "six" people and found that all six can be manipulated. I discovered men and women could change the way they see themselves, change the way others view them, and, in most cases, change *who they really are*.

But before that happens, there has got to be change — real change in the way a person views himself or herself. Only then will he or she change his or her life around for the better. One of my favorite teachers, Mrs. Arthur, drilled it into my head: Your attitude will determine your altitude.

Truer words could not be spoken.

In this book, I will share a few lessons I have learned about courage and why you must have it if you are to be happier than you've ever been. I will also share with you why you must constantly change and evolve to milk all the happiness

FEELING TALL

out of life possible. I hope that if you're like I was years ago, thinking I was never good enough, this book will leave you *Feeling Tall*.

CHAPTER ONE

Others May Look Down on You, But Never Look Down on Yourself

Mirrors Don't Tell the Full Story

All my life, people have reminded me that I am "vertically challenged." That's the politically correct way to say "short."

From my first-grade classroom to the very newsroom I work in today, two things are as unavoidable as taxes and political misconduct: short jokes and tiny humor. I guess I can't blame people for what they see, because in fact I am a short man.

But honestly, I just don't see myself as others appear to see me.

It's almost freakish. Although height is the first thing most people see in me, it's the last thing I see in myself. Some people, however, especially those who think they're clever or those who feel they have to put others down, have no problem with reminding me of my height, or lack thereof.

And believe me, if I've heard one short joke I've heard them all: "Hey Jeff, why don't you take some Vita Grow?" "Hey Jeff, could you loan me a pair of pants? I'm going to the

1

FEELING TALL

beach and I need a pair of shorts!" "How's the weather down there?"

Comments like these usually come from smart aleck seventh-graders whose parents have taught them no better. It was, however, in the eleventh grade — when my science teacher said boys stop growing at 17 — I realized I wasn't going to grow another inch. It was then that I took my first step toward understanding one important variable, a fact that, if forgotten, can make even the most beautiful and intelligent person shrivel to a form of nothing:

You are who you think you are.

It's all about the way you see yourself. I honestly forget how truly short I am. But I do often get subtle reminders. One time in the mid-1990s, for instance, I was youth director for a large church in Harlem. The youth were granted special days to bring in speakers that catered to their needs. Years before, I had met a man who was such an awesome speaker that I decided I had to get him to speak to the kids in my church.

Dr. Richard Barron, a minister and well-renowned youth motivator, agreed to a speaking engagement. On the morning he flew in from Washington, D.C., I met him at LaGuardia Airport in Queens. It was at that meeting I realized that I had psyched myself into believing that I was as tall as anyone else for years.

Dr. Barron is 6 feet 7 inches tall. I'm 5 feet 4 inches. (Well 5-feet-3$^{1}/_{2}$-inches but who's measuring?) I met Dr. Barron at baggage claim and we stopped to have a chat outside the terminal to discuss the weekend events. Dr. Barron is brilliant, so listening to him is one of those rare treats that

Others May Look Down on You, But Never Look Down on Yourself

can distract you from all that is around you. I was not distracted for long.

As we turned to pick up his luggage, we faced a huge window. The glass was either extremely dark or it was covered with one of those black plastic linings. When I faced it, it was as if I was looking in the mirror. It was then I saw it: Dr. Barron looked like a giant, almost as if he were twice my size. His tall frame towered above mine. We looked like a father with his infant son who had just learned to walk. It shocked me so badly I felt like crying. It brought back all the horrible memories of how I was always the smallest boy in class, and on many occasions the smallest person period. The laughs and jokes all came back.

At nearly 31 years old, it was all I could do not to weep bitterly on the way to short-term parking.

Short-Term, boy there's a hard irony. We got in my car and I had a hard time keeping up with the conversation, my mind drifting back to what I had seen in that glass. I drove Dr. Barron straight to the church and then headed straight for the bathroom.

"Get a hold of yourself, Jeff," Then, after pondering it for a while, it hit me: All those years until the point I'd seen myself in the glass with Dr. Barron, I'd thought of him and everyone else who is taller than I am as *my* size and *my* height. I'd spoken to him face to face on many occasions but, surprisingly, I'd never seen a difference before.

In other words, my perception was stronger than my reality. So I straightened up immediately and put my mind at ease. I actually felt pretty good. Dr. Barron had been looking down on me, but I gained great strength in realizing that I had never, ever looked down on myself until that moment.

Up to that point, I'd rarely seen myself next to someone so tall. So in my own mind I was just as tall, just as statuesque as any tall person. You may not have been able to convince

3

FEELING TALL

me otherwise. I perceived myself as someone totally different than what I actually was.

You can do the same thing.

Mirrors are very deceiving. *They don't actually lie,* but they are deceiving. They show what you look like, but they don't reflect the more important image — who you are on the inside and your importance to and potential impact on society. Some look in the mirror and like what they see, but others are repulsed. God bless the people who realize that what they see is not who they really are.

There are many people who act upon the *image* of you. Dr. Barron wasn't like this, but many people do see you and judge you based on what they see. They would have you believe that because they are taller or slimmer than you, or richer or more educated, that you don't have the same ability to thrive as they do — as if you're in a different category.

You know who these people are. The pretty girl at work who has no problem flaunting her body around, has a peanut for lunch and water for dessert, and claims she can't gain any weight. Not all thin people are like this, but you know who I'm talking about.

Or how about the guy who thinks he's so smart that anyone with an opposing view must be crazy. Or what about the tall, dark, and handsome guy who thinks every girl owes him the distinct pleasure of being with him? These people, without saying much, can find a way to insult you or make you feel inferior.

Some people will even test your good nature. They rib you with not so subtle passive-aggressive jabs. Sadly, many of them see you only as a whipping board for their lack of self-confidence.

Others May Look Down on You, But Never Look Down on Yourself

You must not give them the satisfaction.

The trick is to see yourself the way you want to be seen. In other words, whatever your challenge, be it height, beauty, weight, or even intelligence, you're the only one who should judge who you really are.

If you want to be tall, then by God in your mind be tall! I promise you that from the day I saw myself next to Dr. Barron to today, I haven't seen myself as anything but a guy who's just as tall as he is, even at 5-feet-4. This strategy can work for you too.

Here's a promise: If you view yourself in a particular way, others will take note and give you the respect you deserve. People aren't so much impressed with who you are as they are with the aura you convey.

As a television reporter, I interviewed a grandmother in Panama City Beach, Florida who had lost both legs in an accident. Even with that disability, she was able to raise four children and nearly a dozen grandchildren. When I went to interview her, I walked up the stairs to her rickety trailer. It was small but you could tell that, even at its size, it was a house that was built on love and respect for all.

Knowing this woman's situation beforehand, I went into her place with words prepared to comfort her because of her situation. Carefully, I was ready to offer her encouragement. I would tell her that what she'd done was a great accomplishment. I was feeling sorry for her, but she wasn't feeling sorry for herself. She greeted me and my photographer with big, warm hugs. Her dark, leathery hands let me know that she had seen her share of battles and had lost many of them. But the bright light in her eyes was a sign that she was not a victim, but a survivor.

While I interviewed her for our station's Mother's Day special, she made it clear to us that the loss of her legs was a triumph. At first I didn't understand, but she explained that the accident made her *hyper-focus* on things that were really

FEELING TALL

important. In my naïveté I persisted with a line of questioning that I hoped would solicit some form of sadness or sorrow on her part. But it never came to pass. Her words still ring in my ears, "Whatever you do, wherever you find yourself, do your best and the best will come to you." I'd arrived at this woman's house expecting to find someone crippled and discouraged, but instead I'd found a victor.

That's the whole point. You're the only person who can really determine who you really are. Yes, there are people who will size you up or size you down. They'll will execute the box strategy: They'll immediately put you in a box and in their mind, subject you to their rules and their placement, just as I almost did to this grandmother.

What she does every day is what you must do. It's called focus.

When I was growing up, my mother would always read me the Bible. One of the first stories I remember her telling me was the story of David and Goliath, about a small boy who killed a giant. That's as far as many people go. But another look at it reveals that there's so much more.

The story says that Goliath, a giant, was mocking and cursing the nameless and faceless god of David's people. Goliath challenged David's countrymen and fellow warriors to come out from their hiding places and fight like men. Naturally they were all scared of getting creamed, so they hid like the cowards many of them were. Out of nowhere, however, comes David. Biblical historians believe that David was probably no more than 16 years old, that his skin had a funny color, and that he was short for his age.

Others May Look Down on You, But Never Look Down on Yourself

When Goliath saw David, he laughed, got mad and cursed some more. He told David's people that he would break every bone in David's little body and feed them to the animals.

Goliath saw David as a chump; David saw himself as a champ.

Champ or chump: Which are you?

You know the rest of the story: David tells Goliath, "You plan to kill me with a sword, but I will kill you in the name of my god and for my people's sake." Taking one stone, he then **runs** at the giant with no fear.

David knows who he is and what he can do. He's not about to let a loudmouth change the perception he has of himself. He won't let someone who thinks he's superior wreck his feelings of self-worth and importance. He charges at the very thing that has held him down.

David then takes a smooth stone, puts it in his slingshot, and hurls it at the behemoth, hitting him directly in the head. Goliath falls to the floor like a sack of beans. David then takes the giant's sword and cuts his head off. He uses the very weapon that was to be used on him.

David was the best he could be. He had more courage than the more experienced warriors who were fighting on his side. Being the best you can be and having courage and faith in yourself will always bring incredible success. I believe that if you use the methods I describe in this book, you'll be able to overcome even the most difficult of obstacles. I also believe that "weapons" intended to be used on you can become the very tools that clear your pathway to success.

That, my friend, is called believing in who you are and what you can do.

Being a man who is shorter than his counterparts, like David was, I have found one other thing to be true: You cannot handle the real challenges in life with kid gloves,

FEELING TALL

you cannot make light of them, and you cannot deal with them at any time other than right now.

You must deal with challenges swiftly and cleanly, leaving no room for their continued festering growth. If you have a problem with the way you look at yourself, you must attack it and solve it — now.

You must come out with force and change the way you look at yourself.

Need a little help? Do this: Ask yourself the five common but important questions that have challenged mankind from its existence.

- Who am I?
- Where have I been?
- Where am I now?
- What am I doing here?
- Where am I going?

Who am I?

What are you really good at? I mean, what do you enjoy being and doing even if no one asks you or tells you to do it? What do you love? Are you a great quilt maker? Great! Are you a talented interior designer? Are you a fabulous dad or mom? A great writer? A soulful singer? Do you love young people? Are you great at interacting with older people? Whoever you are, be the best at that and everything else will fall into place. The more you work at becoming the best at whatever it is you do, the quicker you will become it. Decide who you are today.

Where have I been?

You've probably heard the warning: *"Those who ignore history are doomed to repeat it!"* This is a

Others May Look Down on You, But Never Look Down on Yourself

hard one. On the one hand, we're encouraged to forget our past, especially if it was negative, and move on to bigger dreams and broader horizons. But reality says that if you don't study the mistakes of your past, you're more likely to repeat them.

That's why you should study your past and make a list, if only a mental one, of the lessons you've learned. Focus only on the outcomes of the lessons, not the lessons themselves. Some lessons might make you cry. But if you focus on what you've learned, you're on your way to making better decisions. Better decision making is the first step toward greatness.

Ask people who have accomplished greatness and they'll tell you they've **made** themselves into the confident people they've become. Yes, there's always the possibility that Michael Jordan is not going to make that last-second shot. Yes, there's a chance that Tiger Woods isn't going to sink that 18-foot putt for eagle. And yes, there's a chance that Mario Lemieux isn't going to score that goal. But if you ask these people about their chances of success, they'll tell you they have no question whatsoever that they can achieve their goals. Why? Because they **think** they can.

Is it possible that they will fail? Of course. But they don't believe it for a second.

They know they can succeed, without a doubt; they are who they think they are.

They know that, when the chips are down, if they can count on no one else they can count on themselves. And believe with every ounce of their being that they are "the go-to person."

That's the way you and I have to be. I know you've got problems with who you are. You may be overweight, a bit geeky looking, or maybe just darn funny looking. Maybe there's something from your past that is holding you back,

FEELING TALL

draining your courage to move forward. But if you can just envision yourself overcoming, then you'll have take the first big step toward actually moving forward. You can be who you are or you can become what you want to be.

People told me I'd never get into television news after spending nine years in accounting. But I saw myself in front of the camera at the scene of a murder or kidnapping, or investigating problems at City Hall. Now I do those things, and much more, everyday. You, too, must start right now down the path to becoming the person you want to be.

Where am I now?

In what condition do you find yourself right now? Determine your current station in life. Are you where you were a year ago? Are you ahead of that point or behind it? Figuring out where you are is a big step in moving forward. An accurate and truthful determination of where you're at is the base from where you must begin. Don't lie to yourself. If where you are stinks, well, admit that. Face it: It's the beginning of the new you.

What am I doing here?

What situation has put you in the place where you find yourself? All of us make bad decisions sometimes. Let's face it: As long as we are humans, we will err. We will choose the wrong friends, we will take the wrong job, and we will listen to the wrong advice that leads down the wrong path. But just as you go down the wrong road sometimes, you can find your way back. Make a U-turn, learn from your mistakes, and never make them again.

Where am I going?

This question does not ask, "*where do I want to go.*" It asks, "If I remain on the current path I'm on, where the heck will I end up?" The fact is that many people are on the wrong track, but they fail to look down the road and see the mediocrity, or even total devastation that awaits them. Wise people take a look not just at the next hour or day, but at the next year or decade. The by tweaking their actions, they pursue greatness. I hope you start tweaking today.

Below is the only exercise in this book, I promise. But I want you to get to the root of who you are and how you can start — right now — becoming the person you know you can be. So:

- Write down the kind person *you* think you are.

- Write down the kind of person you believe *others* think you are.

- Write down the kind of person you *want to be*.

If you know where you're going and you believe you're as "tall" as anyone, you'll never again look down on yourself.

CHAPTER TWO

Underestimate Me ... Please!

Richie Cunningham Never Played So Good

I remember it like it was yesterday. I was the new kid in tenth grade at Lutheran High School East in Cleveland, Ohio. It was a nice school and, for the most part, the students there were friendly. But I knew no one. I'd heard of this school and was looking forward to being accepted. When I entered the school, it was so shiny, so immaculate, and so intimidating. The walls themselves seemed to say *succeed* or *die*.

Although not as tough as a public school, Lutheran East High could be rough, especially for a new kid. I figured as a new *short* kid it had to be worse much, much worse. Yes, there were the awkward stares and those giggles from senior girls who likely said, "Aww, ain't he cute." I didn't tell my mother, but for the first two weeks of the year I had not a soul befriend me.

But all of that changed one day at lunch.

The big senior guys were playing basketball in the gym. As a lowly sophomore, I retreated to my usual corner and began reading my favorite "intellectual" magazine, *MAD*. I was really deep into "Spy Versus Spy" when I heard a bunch of yelling. Nine guys were on the gym floor and wanted to play full court.

They had already picked teams and they needed one more guy. There were other guys in the gym that I had seen play

FEELING TALL

before, but for some strange reason the captain of the team that was one player short called me. He looked all the waydown to the end of the bleachers and said, "Hey, hey little man, come here." I pointed a finger at my own chest and mouthed the word, "Me?" "Yeah. Yeah, little man, come on down here and play some ball." I hesitated and he came to me. "Look, man, I need another guy to play these chumps. Come on down and just run the court with us."

I put down my magazine and slowly walked onto the court. I could hear the other eight guys chuckling. I had on funny-looking jeans, a striped Richie Cunningham ("Happy Days") shirt, and sneakers that certainly were not meant for fashion.

As I walked on the court, the captain said to me, "If you get the ball, don't dribble or shoot, just pass it."

For the first few possessions I didn't even touch the ball; I just ran up and down the court and tried to guard a guy that was about four inches taller than me and extremely quick. No one would pass the ball to me; they didn't think I could handle it. I was not a player in this game.

But something happened that changed all of that. One of my teammates had the ball and was falling out of bounds. He looked around quickly but found no one. He had no choice but to pass the ball to me. I took two dribbles and immediately one of the guys on the other team came charging at me for what he thought would be an easy steal and fastbreak score. Little did he know, I knew the game. I quickly dribbled the ball between my legs and gave him a little fake. He was so surprised, he fell onto the floor behind me.

Underestimate Me ... Please!

I dribbled the ball quickly upcourt and when I got near the basket two other guys approached me. So I went up for a shot. By now the entire gym was watching. As I went up in the air, these guys did too. They were far taller and they knew they had an easy blocked shot. In mid-air I adjusted my body just enough and, with the ball still in my hands, instead of shooting I passed it to a huge teammate who was breaking to the basket. He slam-dunked it home. The people watching went crazy. I was unknown no more. For the rest of that game the guys on my team said, "You're all right, little man."

I'm no Michael Jordan, mind you heck, when it comes to serious basketball I'm not even Michael *Jackson*. But the guys on the opposite team had made a mistake. Because I was small and because they had never seen me play, they thought I would be lunchmeat. They'd underestimated my value. They'd thought that because they were bigger, they were better and they could chew me up and spit me out. Because of that one moment the rest of the school year was a piece of cake.

That's why you should learn to love new situations. In my life's experiences, people always seem to underestimate me. I sit back and watch them, knowing full well that they will probably ignore me and assume I don't have much to contribute. I love to shock them in to the reality that I'm just as smart and just as useful.

By nature, many people like to think that they're better than you. They can't help it. Human nature carries with it an unbelievable superiority complex. Some people need to believe they have something over you, be it that they're taller, have shinier hair, a cuter spouse, a better house, or whatever. And unfortunately, many people will use whatever perceived weakness they feel you have to build themselves up.

As insulting as that is, it can be a good thing; use it to your advantage. It can and will gain you major points when

FEELING TALL

your time comes. Here's why: People who are perceived as nothing gain great attention when they do something well. The trick is that you must be ready with your talent when the time comes. You'll shine and the earth will move for you.

People laugh at loudmouth, arrogant people when they fall on their faces. I'll admit that I too snicker when someone who is self centered and arrogant falters. It is quite the contrary for the person who is underestimated. When the underdog has a victory, the world cheers.

One of my favorite movies is *The Karate Kid*. I still see little Daniel standing in that big auditorium in the crane position. No one believes he can do what he's done, and he beats a big guy in a fight no one would have given him a chance to win. Those are the guys people love and remember.

So when you go to work or school, let the world underestimate you. Keep your mouth shut. Don't talk about your accomplishments; don't brag about where you've been; don't talk about Ph.D. or MD. I didn't get on that basketball court and say, "Hey, man, pass the ball, I'm like Dr. J." (the Michael Jordan of the 70s). Let people think you're the most helpless person in the room. When the time comes, surprise them with your wealth of knowledge or your expertise in whatever it is that you're truly good at.

I've done this dozens of times and it works. Many people I suggest this strategy to have also found success. People like surprises, and when they see that you're more than they bargained for, you garner their instantaneous respect. After my little basketball experience, for example, a girl who otherwise wouldn't have given me the time of day seemed awfully friendly!

Underestimate Me ... Please!

Something similar happened to me while I was living in New York City. I decided I would take a continuing education class in public speaking at New York University. Nearly two dozen people came to class the first night, and although I'd spoken on many occasions I was scared to death. There were at least four lawyers, a couple of corporate vice presidents, and even a couple of actors. All of them had their game faces on, as if to say, "I'm the best here — I have just come to brush up on my skills and crush the rest of you." After the first few minutes of hob-knobbing, it was quite clear to me that I was the only participant who did not do heavyweight communicating for a living.

The instructor was a seasoned veteran in speech. Her instructions were that groups of two people would pair up and introduce each other to the class. I paired up with a big-time bank vice president. This guy had so many credentials it was amazing. He was certified in this and authorized in that and had traveled the world making deals. He was heavy. I was practically the last person to introduce my partner. I walked up to the mic. The podium was so high that all you could see were my head and shoulders. I thought I heard a snicker. Feeling the participants' aura, I sensed they weren't expecting much.

I had them right where I wanted them.

In less than two minutes, I told them the story of this man's life, his love for his children and his commitment to excellence at his bank. I told them he was the husband of one wife and why he ate, slept, and drank success. I was a combination Baptist preacher and courtroom lawyer. One classmate told me afterwards that it was the best introduction of the night. The lady who was next up after me said she didn't want to follow my act.

After the class, the banker I'd introduced said mine were the loveliest words he'd ever heard about himself, and I'd just known him for five minutes. The teacher said, "Jeff, you're a natural."

FEELING TALL

I do hate to brag, and I hate even more to beat up a point. But I was good, and no one was expecting it from me. The teacher told me in private later that I had taken the class to a new level, and that others were trying to reach it.

The fact that people weren't expecting much from me wasn't surprising. Some people look over the vast abyss of humanity and survey. Their minds are so fast and their superiority complexes so set, they begin to eliminate the competition on sight. Without ever hearing you utter a word, they'll put you in one of two boxes: "threat" or "non threat."

You want to be in the nonthreat category. Don't make them sweat. Lull them into a comfortable sense of security. They'll ignore you and virtually leave you alone.

That's fewer headaches for you. But when the time comes, like the Baptist preacher says *you just got to rise up*.

I just love that story of David and Goliath. Goliath thought David was easy prey. In fact, he laughed at this little boy whom he thought he could smash. Goliath just knew he could crush David and send a message to the others that they had better find someone bigger, someone more worthy of his skills, someone better. He charged toward David.

This little guy, the least of them all, had so little going for him. Small guy, no big weapons, no shield, no sword. But he truly believed that, with the supernatural ability given to him, he could do anything. And before the humongous giant could even pull out his sword to slay him, the kid laid him out flat with just one toss from his slingshot.

Underestimate Me ... Please!

Bulls-eye.

Some people may say David was lucky, but I say it was years of whipping that slingshot around like a six-shooter. I think it was David believing in himself and his God-given talents that led him to conclude he could do anything.

Here's where the underestimating principle hits a home run. If that giant had been facing a foe who was just as big as he was, he may have lowered his helmet, or pulled out his bow and arrow more quickly, or lifted his shield higher in preparation for a real battle, some real competition. But since Goliath thought he'd have no problems with the boy, he took that boy for granted. He let his guard down. It's a lesson for all who take things at face value — and for little people with big dreams.

So if people underestimate you, it's really OK. It may be the first step toward slaying the giants on your pathway to success.

CHAPTER THREE

Sometimes a Whippin' Is a Good Thing

Hard Snow Makes a Soft Behind

Back in fifth grade at Ramah Jr. Academy (my elementary school) in Cleveland, we couldn't enter the school until the first bell rang. So all of us who were early had to wait outside in rain, snow, or sleet. Now, if you've ever lived in Cleveland, you know it can get lots of all three. Cleveland has fewer than 87 sunny days all year, on average.

On one particularly cold January morning, everything outside was frozen except my mouth. I was a smart kid in elementary school, and I knew it. A test that I and several of my classmates took in fifth grade showed we were reading on the eleventh grade level. At the time, many of us were smarter than some of the eighth-grade kids. We knew it and they did too.

On that day in the cold, I remember mouthing off to one kid, Joseph New. He was a seventh-grader — a big seventh-grader. I'd overheard him talking about how hard his homework had been the night before. Hearing him describe his difficulties to his classmates, I chimed in, "Aww, man, that stuff is easy." And to me it really was. Here's how stupid I was: I thought Joseph would be so impressed with my command of knowledge that he would beg me, "Please, little smarty pants fifth-grader, share your genius with me so

FEELING TALL

that I too may glean from the wealth therein." His actual words were something like, "I wasn't talking to you midget." "Midget?" I thought. He must be talking to someone else, not someone who was clearly his intellectual superior.

His friends all chuckled.

At this point, what I should have done was lick my little wounded spirit and walk away.

But noooo! I had to respond: "Who you calling a midget? Since you couldn't do your homework, the only thing around here that's a midget is your brain." His friends nearly fell down in laughter. I had to admit, it was a pretty good one for a sniveling kid who hadn't even reached puberty.

Remember, Joe was a big kid — now he was a big kid with a bruised ego. I'd never known him to be violent, but we all know what people are capable of when they feel like they've been pushed too far. Before I knew it, I was hoisted into the air. Somehow, I managed to hang on to my books — don't ask me how. I mean, this guy must have had a gallon of adrenaline or I was super-duper light. He picked me up with only one hand and lifted me to eye level with him. I was so scared I almost wet my pants. (I think I did!) He just stared at me for about five seconds, and an entire crowd stood breathless and silent to see what he would do. I guess the sight of me made him even madder. He lifted me up about three inches higher and threw me across his body into a hard, ice-encrusted snowbank. I hit my head on the ice. My books flew everywhere, and I nearly twisted my arm trying to break my fall.

All the girls ran over to help me up and tried to gather my stuff. One even told Joe off, saying he was nothing more than a great big bully. Somebody told the principal on Joe and he got in a little trouble. Meantime, I learned one of the best lessons of my life that day: Even if you think you're right or smarter than someone, if what you have to say hurts that person's feelings, keep it to yourself. That incident, as painful as it was, has saved me a lot of heartache and has been a great lesson. But what I have to share about it isn't just what I learned, but also *how* I learned it and how you should view your problems.

Believe it or not, problems and messy situations may be among the greatest keys to your success. I learned in one fight (although it wasn't much of a fight) what it might have taken me years to learn otherwise: *Shut up when you don't have to talk.*

Many people have the distinct and misguided notion that obstacles are bad things. Quite the contrary: Obstacles are the very things that give you strength, speed, and knowledge. I can't tell you how many times since that day in the schoolyard that I have kept something to myself that I knew was true but that might have hurt or embarrassed someone. If you take a good look at them, tough times can teach you a lot. Some situations are not just tough but downright cruel. So many times I've just been in the wrong place at the wrong time and something bad has happened to me. I call them *tragedy's tough reminders*, and I vow to never do the same thing or be in the same place ever again. Fool me once shame on you; fool me twice, shame on me.

My mother always said, "Hard times don't last always." But when you're in the middle of a hard time, it seems as if it will never go away. The hurt, the anguish, and the pain all seem like they'll remain as scar tissue of your incident or trial forever. I want to let you know that your hard time will end. I also promise that if you learn from it, it was worth it.

I once heard a preacher say, "Either you're going into a trial, you're in the midst of a trial, or you're just coming out of a trial. Learn from it."

FEELING TALL

People who already feel they're on the outside often find themselves facing some sort of personal problem. They believe others are making light of them, perhaps laughing at them, because they're nerdy or overweight or very skinny. Whatever the problem, those who think they're superior often give these people a hard time. Here's a news flash for those verbal or emotional trials —learn something. Sometimes the things people say are hurtful, but they may also be a vehicle of change for your betterment.

We had a family of kids in our elementary school who walked around with a strange body odor all day. The teachers spoke to them and we teased them behind their backs, but they made no change. The odor wasn't unbearable but it was strong and noticeable. It wasn't until a Christmas gift exchange that the family finally got the message. Someone picked the name of the oldest girl in the family to purchase a gift for. The person could have bought the girl a little radio or something cute. But to the girl's horror, the person who picked her name bought her towels, a bar of soap, and some deodorant.

The teacher could do nothing; the box was already opened, the contents revealed.

The girl was ashamed and beyond mortified, and the message was sent. The giver of this needed but embarrassing gift was reprimanded, but the deed was done. The girl was hurt and humiliated, but be that as it may, the gift worked. The girl's strange odor disappeared. She must have used the stuff. It was a horrible psychological and emotional beating for her, but the message had come through loud and clear. It had been a great step for her in the right direction. She had learned from her trial.

Sometimes a Whippin' Is a Good Thing

There are other great outcomes from trials. There are those of us who may not be as rich as some, or as tall, or as good looking. There are easy targets for people who randomly issue harsh criticisms. When people are scared to fight the good competition, they fight the fights they know they can win. That's what many cowards do.

What many people are thinking about people like you and me is that we're easy marks. But our frequent challenges give you and me another advantage to do things others don't do: practice. Practice affords you the ability to duck and weave and punch just at the right moment. It strengthens your workout and helps you build up your defenses. The challenges you're going through right now, believe it or not, are going to make you tougher, smarter, and one heck of an opponent. So instead of cowering when faced with adversity, get strong and build your courage and resolve. It will take you a long way.

I once heard a gold specialist tell the story of how gold is purified. In the flotation method of purifying gold, the precious metal has to go through lengthy processing. First, it is heated at extreme temperatures. This is done to break down the gold and separate the good in the gold from the bad. When the gold has reached the optimum temperature, a small layer of impurities can be seen on top. Slowly and carefully that layer is scraped off. The gold is then allowed to sit and cool, only to then be poured into a different container to start the process all over again. More boiling, more scraping, more cooling off, then pouring again. This is done over and over again until there is barely any residue left on top. The resulting material then becomes the gold that is molded and sold on the open market. The gold is poured from vessel to vessel until it's perfect. The rough parts now gone, only the best remains.

This analogy has an obvious but fundamentally important message to those who truly seek success: *Things get better by first getting worse.* Great corporate leaders are not cho-

FEELING TALL

sen because they were handed the world on a silver spoon (at least not most of them). The great majority of successful private and public industry leaders are chosen because they've gone through great trials and have turned their organizations around. It's never easy, but it teaches them much about handling others and turning onions into onion rings.

I'm not wishing anything bad on you, nor do I suggest that you rejoice when you face adversity. But you would do well to take a good, hard look at how you can personally grow from your trials. As a child, I was teased, picked on, and laughed at. Those experiences fueled my need to succeed and prove wrong everyone who ever thought of me as weak or as an underachiever. I have the news awards to prove I've done well.

Without debate, life is tough. But in spite of that reality, many people still find a way to climb to the top.

Actor Sidney Poitier is an example of what a person can do when focused and faced with a trial. Poitier was born in Miami to immigrant tomato farmers in 1927. He had only two years of formal education, from ages 11 to 13. As a young adult, he moved to New York City and had a great desire to become an actor. But because of his thick West Indian accent, he was passed over for role after role after role. Living basically in squalor, Poitier read and taught himself to speak without the accent. After years of trying to land roles, he finally got his start and went on to become the first African American actor to win an Academy award. It happened in 1963 for his role in *Lilies of the Field*. Was it easy? Of course not. Was his road littered with obstacles? Certainly. Were there people telling him to give up and do something else?

Sometimes a Whippin' Is a Good Thing

Without question. But learning from his dilemma and understanding what was keeping him from his goals, he turned his whippin's into successes and has gone on to a distinguished career in acting.

In 1996, he told a newspaper:

> "No one ever expected the son of a tomato farmer and a semi-literate lady to ever make any stir of consequence. I flirted with reform school. I was an incorrigible kid to some extent. I didn't know where I was, who I was, or what I was. And the society in which I lived didn't care too much."

I've had the pleasure of meeting Mr. Potier and he's a great guy, who never let anything hold him down.

What dilemma has got you down? What horrible situation is beating you so badly that you're not actively pursuing your goals? Is it a failed marriage? An abusive childhood? The fear you may not be smart enough or good enough? Have you been teased so much about your weight or looks that you feel no one will be interested in whatever you have to offer? Whatever beating now weighs upon your soul, let that be the very thing that catapults you into your finest hour. All the abuse you've taken ... let it be the thing that moves you to move on, and let an old adage carry you upon it's wings: *"Tough times don't last; tough people do."*

So don't let a tough past or hard times cripple you from sailing out onto the seas of success. Remember that you have what it takes to move forward. Yes, you may indeed be smarting from a past experience. Or you may be hurting from something you're going through right now. Learn from it and make sure it never happens again. Then file it under "lessons learned" and step out into the cool breeze of what will surely be the best days of your life.

CHAPTER FOUR

Face the Facts and Move Forward

Take a Good, Long Look

ntrospection is a word I learned in Mrs. Arthur's sixth grade class. I love the word. It may be the most valuable word in the English language.

Random House dictionary describes it this way:

Introspection — The examination of one's own mental and emotional state.

I like that definition, but here's mine.

Jeff Williamson's definition:

Introspection — The total examination of self and what you have or don't have to offer to society.

I like my definition better and I'll tell you why.

I come from a family of five boys. I'm the middle, number three. My father, who was good with his hands, was probably exhausted when he got to me. That's because he trained my two older brothers to be great with **their** hands. They can take apart engines, do major renovations in their homes, and fix just about anything, just like my father. But me? I can barely tighten a doorknob without checking online or going to the hardware store to figure out how to

FEELING TALL

do it. I'm just not built that way. My late Uncle Marshall would tell me, "Boy, you're all brains no brawn."

He was right. I'm just not good at those things and I never have been. Oh, I've enjoyed a few things since childhood, and since buying a home recently I've learned to do basic household maintenance out of necessity. But I still stay ten feet from a car engine. I've never even changed my own oil. I used to be ashamed of that, but no longer.

When I take a good, long, introspective look, I realize that repairing cars is just not for me. So I'm not going to force it. I also like to sing, but I'm not so good at that either. So I'll only do it in the shower. I also just learned, after eight years, how much I hated accounting, my first career. I thought it was my road to success, but I couldn't have been more wrong. Learning who I am and who I am not has been worth more than gold. It's a lesson you too must learn if your life is to progress.

Like I used to be, many people are unhappy. They're like fish out of water because they haven't taken a good look at who they are. They operate based on surface needs and don't look and dig deep. Many don't investigate who they want to become, either.

I can't understand why. Isn't happiness the goal of life? Isn't that what we should be striving for? Don't you want bliss? So why, then, are there so many people out there who have never taken a good internal peek to see what really makes them tick and what they get excited about? How many people do you know who sit back in the same mundane jobs, day after day, and move nowhere? They complain that they're unhappy, yet they do nothing to change. Why not take some time every day and figure out what makes you grin and feel all mushy inside?

I've come to the conclusion that I'm a short guy who will never play in the NBA. I'll never win the long jump competition, and I'll certainly never be the first one to know it's raining (another stupid joke from hecklers). I've always wanted to dunk a basketball. Back in high school, at only 5-feet-4 I amazed my classmates when I jumped high enough to touch the rim. As the young kids say, back then I had "ups." But those dreams are gone, and now I just dream of shooting under 100 on the golf course. I'm a terrible golfer, but maybe one day, with enough practice, my swing will improve. The point is, there are some things you will never be. And let's face it: Many people are spinning their wheels everyday trying to be something that they're not. It's like trying to fit a square peg in a round hole: It will never happen.

I can hear the critics now: "C'mon, Jeff, figuring out who you are is in total contradiction with your "you are who you think you are" admonition in Chapter One. Quite the contrary; it's the continuation. I've never believed in putting anyone in any box. But the truth is that many of us are forcing activities in a field. We've literally forced ourselves to believe we have to do what we do. We feel this way sometimes because we feel trapped financially, worn out physically, or too darn scared to make any change that will upset the delicate fruit basket that is our lives. But guess what: fruit has a way of growing back.

I know that because it happened to me.

In high school and in junior high, I was always an ace in math. I don't know why. It was one of those things that came naturally to me. So my friends and even older people in my church told me it would be a good idea to go into accounting when I got to college.

Much of the collegiate literature of the time suggested that accounting was the hottest field, second only to chemical

FEELING TALL

engineering. So by golly, when I got to college I said, "*Sign me up for that accounting major.*" It should have been a sign to me in the first semester, when I got a D in Accounting 101, that the field was not for me. Little did I realize that accounting had little to do with math. But I kept forcing myself into a space that did not fit. Class after class, my grades proved I was misplaced. A C here, a C- there. I suppressed my true distaste for accounting and my love for the required communication classes all students had to take. I truly enjoyed going to speech class and English class but never took the time to understand why. Maybe it's because I was always taught to stick with things and they will soon get better. That philosophy has merit. But since I was sticking to something I didn't love and therefore couldn't get to work for me, the theory fell apart. I was very similar to the person who stays with the abusive spouse, hoping things will get better and unquestioning when they never do. After a while, I got tired of the self-abuse and had to run.

After graduating with just so-so grades, I took a series of jobs that completely let me and those I worked for know that accounting was not my forte. For years, I was lost in a career in which I felt trapped and helpless. It was not until ten years later that I knew I had to change.

One cold morning in New York, I woke up and went into the shower. In there, I daydreamed of giving a great motivational speech to thousands of people who felt they were lost in their jobs and in their lives. The speech just flowed off my lips. My wife, who has always thought that I'm a little crazy, heard me talking to myself and promised once again to have me committed. She teased me, but she knew all too well that I was indeed lost.

Face the Facts and Move Forward

She knew I was smart and talented, but that I couldn't find the vehicle that would transport me to happiness.

As I was showering, recent events came to my mind. About two years prior, some friends had asked me to emcee their wedding reception in Bermuda. Accountants are supposed to be bland loners, not masters of ceremonies. Shocked at the request, I took the job and had a great time. Apparently, the couple saw something in me I did not see in myself. There were a few people in the audience who were getting married. They were so impressed with the job I did that they asked me to emcee their weddings as well. I've been to dozens of weddings since then and I emceed most of them — not to mention parties and galas for other organizations.

The realization of what I'd been doing at all of these events came to me as I finished my dazzling morning shower speech. It was then I knew that I had to leave nine years of accounting behind and move on to greater heights. Not that accounting isn't a lofty calling; quite the contrary, accountants serve a function that is needed in every venue in the world. But introspection led me to understand that it wasn't for me, and I wasn't going to do it one more day than I had to.

While still working in accounting, I enrolled in a master's class in speech communications at New York University. Words cannot express how much I loved the program and the professors. It was that degree that led me into television news, a field that has brought me more satisfaction and awareness in seven years than I learned in ten years of accounting.

Thank God I faced the facts and moved forward. I'm a happier now than at any other time in my life.

Don't get me wrong: I was scared. I knew I'd have to start from the bottom and work my way up. But I was going nowhere, and time wasn't stopping while I peeked at options. I had to diligently explore those options and make

FEELING TALL

changes. This realization came only after I had faced myself with the true prognosis of my condition: My life was a career flatline. And so I had to face myself, determine what made me happy, and make a real change.

Where are you and what's holding you back? And what do you have within you to make you move forward?

Taking a look at yourself and seeing where you really are can be painful. My look back nearly tore me apart. Your introspection may be just like mine and reek of time wasted and a life of mediocrity or just plain failure. But I want to let you know that, by taking a close and hard look at where you are and what your true talents are, you can be everything your heart desires — if you make an effort to change now. The introspective look should give you clues as to what you can do that will maximize your talents.

You might ask, "How do I find that thing that is deep within that will put me on the road to true happiness and success?" I'm betting for you that it will be as clear as it was for me. I call it the *shower experience*.

Every single one of us has a place where we dream. For some, it's the shower in the morning, where a dream may consist of brokering a big deal. Others may dream on a park bench at lunch of opening a flower shop. Some may even dream in the car while waiting for the kids to come out from school. But if you look at your past week, I'll bet you can pinpoint a place where — and, likely, a time when — everything else stands totally still and your dream comes to life in living color.

That's the place where the reality of what you love meets the wherewithall of your capabilities. That special place of dreams and the times you have them should not be taken lightly. It's there that you find your love of life and the answers to many of life's questions. Find that place and dream your dream. Let that dream take you to a better place in your life.

In my first television news job for the NBC affiliate in Panama City Beach, Florida, I met the most incredible person. He was a teenager by the name of Tommy. One day, Tommy came home from school with his brother and went right to bed. He complained of aches and pains and said he was going to lie down for a few minutes. His brother said OK and left him to hang out with friends. Tommy told me he started to feel hotter and hotter as he lay in bed that day, and by the time he realized he was in trouble he couldn't move his hands or legs to call for help. His doctor later said that if someone had been there to help him within the first hour or so, he would have been fine. But several hours passed before Tommy's parents got home and realized their son was in a coma.

Later that night at the hospital, they heard the unthinkable news their son had been diagnosed with meningococcal septicemia, or meningitis, and that in time doctors would have to amputate both of his legs and arms if he was to live. After getting the green light from his parents and his doctor, I was given permission to interview Tommy about his tragedy. I went to the hospital thinking I would find a teen who was very down on himself. I got quite a shock. Tommy was more upbeat than I was. He sat in his wheelchair and, with the most uplifting voice, he said, "This thing's got me,but it didn't *get* me. And I can either feel sorry for myself or I can go on with my life."

That's what I call introspection.

Tommy realized that, yes, his life wasn't going to be what he'd planned for it to be. Yes, he was different from others. He faced himself and his situation and found them both to be grim. But after that cold, hard look, he knew he had

FEELING TALL

changes to make and that he would move on toward greatness. He is now very much a self-sufficient person and happier than most people with two legs and two arms. He spends mch of his time encouraging teens and others to be happy with life.

You, too, have a choice. After you take a good look at yourself, you'll realize that where you are is not where you have to stay. And if you're in a good situation, you can still make it better. I'm in my fourteenth year of marriage, and I think my wife and I are just starting to figure out where we've come from. After taking a good look at everything there is about us, we've learned where we're going.

I know it may frighten you, but find that secret place and let your mind flow to the haven of your ultimate success. There, you will take the first step toward a new and richer life. This is the beginning of realizing what will bring you ultimate happiness.

Growing up, I remember people telling me that the first step to solving a problem is realizing you have one. Take a long, hard look inside, identify your joy, find your dream, and go after it.

CHAPTER FIVE

Be Tough, but Nice

The Fight without a Punch

Sounds like an oxymoron, right? How in the world can you be tough and nice at the same time? Let's start with tough.

Once you've established yourself and begun moving in the direction of your dream, you'll still be the underdog. The person who considers himself or herself the favorite will still believe he or she can kick you around. To circumvent that, you must carry yourself in a way that lets others automatically know you're not one to be messed with. If it takes a David and Goliath experience for that to happen, so be it.

Back in seventh grade at Alexander Hamilton Junior High School, there was a nerdy kid in my class whose name was Obie. I'll never forget about a fight that *did not happen* and the respect that ensued immediately. I call Obie nerdy because he wore big, thick, black horn-rimmed glasses and striped shirts every day. He walked with a little bounce and always sat at the front of the room. Being a short guy with not so many friends myself, I made it my business to get to know this kid. After meeting him I found him to be quite a nice guy. He was smart, funny, and a joy to be around. But I think I was the only one who knew that.

One day in history class, one of the school bullies started in on poor Obie, and it wasn't the first time. You know the type — tall and popular, the bully that terrorized everyone.

FEELING TALL

But he really was a thug who picked on people like Obie and sometimes me. When the history teacher turned his back, this bully, Carl, threw a pencil and nailed Obie with the sharp end right in the back of his neck. Obie careened in pain and stood up and faced the class. After all the mess he'd been through, the name calling, the teasing, he'd had enough. He said, "Carl, you punk, I know you did that!" Carl, insecure person that he was, certainly could not back down from the fight.

He said, "Yeah, I did it. So what?" Obie said nothing but stared at Carl as if he had the power to dismantle him with his eyes.

The teacher objected and told the boys to cool off. Carl said, "I'm going to kick your butt after class," pointing to Obie. We all knew Obie was a goner.

When the bell rang, Obie was the first one out the door. I breathed a sigh of relief, thinking Obie had come to his senses and had run home to his momma. But to my amazement and disbelief, I found Obie outside the classroom, pocket protector off, school bag on the floor, fists balled up in the air, and with a look of utter destruction on his face. At that point, as mad as he was, I believe Obie could have beaten Joe Frazier.

When Carl came out, you should have seen the look on his face. He, too, thought Obie was a coward and a chump. Even if Obie had been both, Carl knew he had a fight on his hands and one he could easily lose. Obie was taking his stand.

Carl was white as a sheet. He looked at Obie and took a half-step toward him. Obie tightened his fists, and boy did his forearm look huge for that of a seventh-grader. It was then that Carl did perhaps the wisest thing that he'd ever done. With seem-

Be Tough, but Nice

ingly the whole school watching, he chuckled awkwardly at Obie, as if to say, "you're not worth my time." He then turned and walked away. Kids who had been terrorized by Carl in the past cheered. There was finally a victory for the underdogs.

There comes a point in your life when you have to take a stand. You just have to. It doesn't have to happen often, but there's got to be a time when you get tough. People respect people who take a stand on issues and on themselves. The fact is that some people don't expect you to take a stand at all. Most people who think they're smarter than you or better than you believe that whenever there's an issue or conflict, you'll fold on it. They believe you'll succumb to their will. Sometimes that will be the right thing to do, because others can be right sometimes. But don't think that you're a second-class citizen and that you must always concur with others. You, too, have a voice, and you should make it be heard loud and strong, especially when the subject of the discussion is near and dear to your heart.

In fact, I have come to the overwhelming conclusion that those who longingly watch from the sidelines are usually the ones with the best ideas. It's because they listen. People who are always talking cannot be listening. They aren't paying attention to the full spectrum that's around them. That's why many CEOs make sure they have personal assistants who listen and observe the environment — "paid listeners," if you will, that report information back to them. You should never be afraid to voice your thoughts with confidence and strength. You are the person who could turn the tide at work, at church, or at home. Let your voice be heard, even if it seems to some that you're being annoying. When you do decide to speak up, some people will be surprised and think it's cute. There are others, however, who will think that what you have to say is worthless, and they'll be mad that you're even opening your mouth. But life is short; why should you keep everything bottled up and

FEELING TALL

stuck down inside? Whatever you've got, say it, and do so with tough confidence.

I have to admit that sometimes I get a little carried away. When I encounter someone new, be it a salesperson or someone else, I think the person has already sized me up and figures I'm either a sucker or too shy to speak my mind. When I get that feeling, I make sure the first words out of my mouth are ones that command respect.

I'll even raise my voice just a bit so that there is no question I'm a person to be reckoned with, and that trying to pull the wool over my eyes is a major mistake. I sometimes even create a miniscene if my suspicions appear to be correct. It's the first and last mistake the people I'm dealing with ever make.

However, as much as you need toughness, you also must have an equal portion of kindness. One of the best bosses I've ever had was a person you wouldn't want to disappoint because she was so tough, but whom you also wanted to support because she was so nice. If you did something wrong, she would let you know. She hated slothfulness, irresponsibility, and non-creativity. If you were guilty of any of these, she'd tell you; but if you were found to have done something above and beyond the call of duty, she'd hug you and squeeze you half to death. To be successful, it's important to learn how to balance love and judgment fairly.

Without kindness, just being tough all the time makes you a jerk — a big jerk. Yes, you can congratulate yourself, patting yourself on the back when you have intimidated or threatened someone into doing what you want. But if you have no mercy to balance your justice, you are the loser. And when things are not going well for you, the same people

Be Tough, but Nice

you climbed on, will watch you fall and will even help you fall. I've seen it a hundred times.

The fact is, we need each other. While you shouldn't allow your opinions to be overlooked, you also shouldn't try to make your voice the only one heard.

A wise man once told me, "I've never seen a man on his deathbed say, 'I wish I'd squashed that guy.'" Invariably, people on their deathbeds are thinking, "Boy, this hospital room sure is empty!" Kindness and the Golden Rule should be at the forefront of all decisions. They are the linchpins upon which all other issues turn.

I learned about kindness as a child. Growing up in a family of five boys and one TV, things could get a bit contentious. I mean, how could tempers not flare when you're deciding whether to watch *Gilligan's Island* or *Hogan's Heroes*? That isn't an easy choice. My brother David and I wanted to hear Sergeant Schultz say, "I see *nuthink*" but my other brothers, Eric and Gerald, wanted to see the Skipper beat up Gilligan with his hat. I mean, these fights were heated — but I digress.

We'd fight over anything. But if my father was around, the fights would end quickly. He was a tough disciplinarian. But he worked so hard that breaking up fights became my mother's duty.

Sometimes I noticed she would just let us beat each other's brains out and learn our own lessons. But most of the time, she'd stop us and admonish us with words I have come to live by: *"Boys, boys, learn to be kind."* These are words that everyone, male or female, short or tall, black or white, could live by: "Learn to be kind."

To look at it from a reverse perspective, those who are truly kind **are** being tough. Huh? I once witnessed a boss of mine who fired an employee after warning him about his temper. The guy really had a bad one. The employee, who was a photographer, would criticize reporters in front of crowds

FEELING TALL

and challenge his bosses at meetings. He was a guy who couldn't control his temper. After carefully documenting the employee's other offenses, the news director told the photographer to go home on day after he came back from a story. The photographer was given two weeks pay and sent on his way. His face registered shock and utter disappointment.

I asked the news director the next day if he felt bad about the firing. He said, "Jeff, it was an act of kindness on my part." "Kindness?" I said. He continued, "If I let him think he can belittle everyone he comes in contact with, one day he'll meet the wrong person to tangle with. And then it could be more important than a news job it could be his life. So while he'll struggle for a while, I hope this will help him make a change for the better."

Being kind is often harder than being tough. Any hothead or spoiled brat can lose his or her temper when things don't go the "right" way. But it takes a person with real courage and wisdom to know when to hold back and say words that mend and heal.

My wife often tells me I have a Napoleonic complex — the short guy who doesn't like people messing with him. But she also tells me I'm the sweetest guy on Earth. The truth is that you have to be both. It's a weird tightrope, but after you learn to walk it, people will respect you, love you, and believe in your vision.

By the way, Obie — the nerdy guy with the striped shirt who got into a near fight with Carl the bully — said very little about the confrontation afterwards. No bragging, no machismo; he let his fists and his stand do all the talking. All through junior high he was one of the nicest guys I had the privilege to know.

CHAPTER SIX

Get Ahead of the Crowd

Carry the Gear... and Like It!

In order to be ready when you make your transformation into the powerful person you will soon be, you have to start preparing now. You can be as tough as you want or you can be as nice as Edith Bunker, but when the time comes for you to shine and you're not ready, it's an opportunity wasted.

That's why, starting today, this very hour, you must strive for excellence. You must become the *best of the best.* Be like the character in the show *The Six Million Dollar Man*: *better, stronger, faster* — **smarter.** This takes time and commitment and utter perseverance. Forget overnight fixes. Those who have sat on the outskirts watching others enjoy life must eat, sleep, and drink methods of self-improvement: Every day, you must practice something new and ingrained in you must be the voice of inner confidence: "I can do anything." You have to believe it and make those you *used* to depend on now depend on you.

You've got to be better than the best person who does what you do. Getting ahead of the crowd means that people look beyond whatever makes you different from them, seeing only the excellence you now deliver on a daily basis. Getting to this level takes several important steps: working,

FEELING TALL

planning, and strategizing while everyone else is asleep. You may have kids, a demanding schedule, even a demanding spouse, but you've got to find time to get ahead of the crowd.

Average is just not good enough. And I should know about average.

I'll never forget when I ended my career in accounting and decided I wanted to pursue television news. Friends who were in the business told me it's a field like any other: It takes time to develop within it and become a top-notch reporter. Skilled reporters are hard to come by. It's a career that takes precision, great research and interviewing skills, and the ability to operate under pressure and remain smooth on camera. Developing contacts and creating thought-provoking stories are the heart of success.

News directors hire television reporters, and NDs aren't the most patient people in the world. They expect you to walk in the door having contacts and great stories. They want the learning curve to be minimal. The only question they really want you to ask when hired is, "Where's the bathroom?"

When I walked into station WJHG-TV, an NBC affiliate in Panama City Beach, Florida, high expectations met me there. In such a small town, viewers know you're going to make on-air mistakes. But station chiefs want them to be few.

My station was the number one station in town, and it had no plans to surrender to the ABC affiliate, the number two news station. Though well trained when I came in the door, I was intimidated. In news markets that size, you're usually a one-man band. That means you're your own photographer, sound person, reporter, and film editor.

Get Ahead of the Crowd

And let me tell you, you've never lived until you've carried a 25-pound tripod, a 30-pound camera, and a light kit (a.k.a. "the gear") up four flights of stairs. For a little guy like me it wasn't always easy.

Having been in a different career for so long, it took me a long time to get adjusted. Too long. I was a 33-year-old man competing with 22-year-olds who were stronger and didn't have three kids and a wife at home like I did. But I made it my business to be just as good as, if not better than, every reporter in that market. I stayed late every night trying to understand the nuances of editing tape. I asked those who were good at shooting footage to teach me how to do it better. I would come in early and stay late almost every day. I did so without getting paid for much of the overtime.

At home, I would take articles from the newspaper and rewrite them in television news form. I studied story after story and watched dozens of reporters. The analysis of their writing and on-camera performance became my life. Day by day, I got better and everyone noticed. It didn't take long for many of the big stories to find their way to my desk, and for me to become *the* reporter for many special assignments.

Since then, I have won several awards for excellence in reporting. I chalk it up not to talent or intelligence but to good old elbow grease and hustle. It works every time.

In order for me to get ahead of the crowd, it took diligence that many would shun. There is a saying, "The race is not to the swift, but to him that endures until the end." Success is measured not in miles but in inches. People who work on their skills every day, even if just for a few minutes, are the people who receive the prizes. Skill has its place, but perseverance kicks rear end. Just by chewing a bit of your goals everyday, working hard, and becoming adept at what you do, excellence becomes the norm.

I once saw Michael Jordan being interviewed on TV. The reporter asked him where he got his great basketball abilities.

FEELING TALL

Jordan turned to the reporter and said, "I just work out so hard every day so that what my hands and feet do are automatic." In other words, when he's in a tough situation, he doesn't really have to think about what to do. Since he's practiced so much, his senses basically go on autopilot. And that gives him the edge.

That's the way you have to become — so quick with knowledge, so fast with information that people realize you're the man or the woman! Carry your knowledge not with arrogance or conceit but with a sense of pride, knowing you've put your time in behind the scenes.

The ability to achieve excellence is not easy to come by; it takes patience. Many people become frustrated when they can't get ahead fast enough. They want it all or nothing at all. They want success to drop directly into their laps. This is popular sentiment but poor strategy. The few people at the top of their respective fields haven't gotten there by happenstance but by hard, gritty, consistent planning and goal setting.

Here are three additional strategies that will help you get ahead of the crowd:

Pay attention.

To gain power and influence with others, you have to know who the players are. You also have to figure out how others in the same environment have become successful. Do you remember when you were a kid and were told to stop, look, and listen before crossing the street? The same advice applies here. People who truly pay attention to what's going on are less likely to get hit by a truck. They'll also be the ones with valuable information that can move them forward.

Set reasonable goals

Limited goals help keep down your frustration and raise the level of your consciousness slowly. Experts say the best way to learn is slowly but consistently. Let's say you've always wanted to write a book or learn to sing. Start off slowly. Take one class and see how you do. If you're writing a book, buy a cheap journal and write each day. Let the beginnings of a new undertaking be on a slow boil, then dive in and learn all you can. It's important that you don't worry about how long it will take you. Plan time to work on your project every day. We all like to be ahead in the race, but to speed up you need to slow down. In the end, the race is really only something you have against yourself. Setting goals also helps you keep your eye on the prize; every day, you'll chip away at what will be your ultimate success.

Envision victory

All of your goal setting should be aimed at an ultimate achievement. What is it for you? To go back to school and get your master's degree or Ph.D.? Maybe it's to get a high school diploma. Paint a picture in your head of yourself in that cap and gown, with your family going nuts in the audience. See yourself taking that diploma and shaking the campus president's hand. Maybe you want to be reporter like me. See the lead anchor tossing viewers out to you as you go live from a raging inferno with thousands of people watching. Let your daily goal setting be fueled by a dream. Nothing, and I mean nothing, is better than working toward a goal and then having it actually happen. And it can! You just have to make it your daily business to *just do it*. Nike coined the phrase, but you can make it yours.

This is the most important step of all. There is a Biblical saying, "Without a vision, the people perish." You will never get ahead of the crowd if you don't keep the prize in front of you. Let's face it; there are a thousand people like you who want what you want. But I promise you that,

FEELING TALL

almost every time, the person who wins the prize is the person who lives the dream daily and works at it consistently. To that person is bestowed the honor and the title of "winner."

And don't be fooled: Some people will react negatively when they see the transformation. "Who does she think she is?" they will ask. "He's getting too big for his britches," they will retort. Make sure you build up the resolve to not let words bother you. Some people are just downright jealous. As soon as they see you transforming, many of them will become petty. Some people can't stand to see others climb the ladder of success, so they'll try to tear you down each time you advance up a rung. Ignore them. Do what you have to do to become successful and move ahead of all others.

If you're anything like me, you need every advantage you can possibly get. The more you stay ahead, the more the power you'll ultimately yield. When you get there — and you will get there — *stay there*!

I played on the basketball team in high school. We were great at getting a lead, but after we got ahead we felt comfortable and started playing sloppy. In the end, the opposing team would often catch up and we'd lose the game. Had we kept up the intensity and hard work, we could have held them at bay. But instead we fizzled out, like a cheap sparkler on the Fourth of July. That is the lesson for you, my friend: Never give up the helm once you've got it. It's great to get a fast start, and for those who do I congratulate them. But make sure you resolve in your mind to have a fantastic finish. When you get to the top, study harder, think faster, and create an even larger space between you and the next person. Work so hard that others will never get a chance to catch up. Carry your gear and like it.

CHAPTER SEVEN

Paint Your Picture for the World

Whatever Is Inside of You, Get It Out

We're not talking exorcism here. Well, maybe we are. The fact is that everyone has a God-given talent. It's something that comes from within, and if it's not already out it's dying to get out. Since you're reading this book, chances are you know that. Hiding deep within you is a love that has been squashed.

For years, I worked in accounting. After ten years in the field, I came to the conclusion that I hated it. I disliked everything about it. It even made me dislike many of the people I worked for. I was miserable and my family and friends knew it.

I was cooped up in an office day after day after day. Now, for some people that's a good thing. They love to work alone. They love special projects that allow them to distance themselves from others. Great! But that's just not me. There was another guy walking around in my head, held prisoner by the sheer limitations he had put on himself. He was rattling the bars on the cell, but I wouldn't let him out. I found release in other areas.

FEELING TALL

Sometimes when I would write reports or be asked to speak at my church or emcee a wedding or concert, I felt totally in my element. I would plan and prepare for weeks for one speech or one concert. But then I would get in front of the crowd and not use my prepared material at all, my natural instincts would take over.

Even before I got into television news, I would host dozens of concerts, emcee scores of weddings, and do so much more with my natural gift of communication. After getting into news, organizations from all over asked me to make speeches and moderate panels.

Thanks to a conscious decision on my part to let that "other guy" in my head free, I'm the happiest man alive. Am I making lots of money? No, not *yet*. Am I a Pulitzer Prize winning writer? I've won a few awards, but the Pulitzer will have to wait. But boy oh boy am I happy! Happiness breeds success and forces you to get better and better at whatever it is you do. Along the way, you find people who help you do things even better and encourage you.

I have lots of friends who are doctors, lawyers, politicians. They're riding high on their successes. I begrudge them nothing. I've learned to celebrate right along with them. I praise them when they do well. In fact, the more I hang around success, the more I press toward it myself.

You should do the same.

Stop hanging around people who have held you down; they'll only drag down to their level. My fifth-grade teacher, Mrs. Jenkins, would tell us, "If you're gonna soar with the eagles you can't run with the turkeys." Find successful people and

Paint Your Picture for the World

make them your friends and role models. You'll change your whole outlook in doing so.

In fact, the best way to live your dreams is to hang around people who are living theirs.

My friend Hallerin Hilton Hill is a good example of someone living his dream and achieving success. He's got the number one morning news talk show in the state. This guy can make you believe you can walk on water. Whenever we have a chance to do lunch or even have a quick conversation, he makes me responsible for my dreams. If you say you're going to do something positive, whenever he sees you he says, "How's the project coming?" A successful songwriter, speaker, and author, his presence fuels my engine of success. His book, *Seven Pillars of Wisdom,* is as uplifting as he is. It chronicles seven tasks you must master or perform if you are to truly become happy in life and in love. Hanging around Hallerin and others like him is one of the main reasons I had the courage to write this book.

Courage is something I learned while changing careers. While still in accounting, I really struggled with what my alternatives were. But I decided it was time for me to look at my situation because I was at a crossroads.

I had to make a change. Change hurts. It's hard. I should know. I mean, any guy who changes from being an accountant to becoming a television reporter ought to know about change. I hate making changes, but there comes a time when you have to seek true enlightenment, self-enlightenment. I'm not talking about some mystical experience; I'm talking about living life from a perspective of sheer happiness. My change gave me not only a new look at a long-term perspective, but also a reason to wake up in the morning and do something new and fresh each day.

There are so few people who wake up happy and content every morning. But those who do find that happiness isn't what they do, but being happy in what they do. Many people

FEELING TALL

have learned a simple lesson: Happiness is the ability to express yourself in a way that creates energy all by itself.

There are so many people out there who think they'd be truly happy if they won the lottery. But I've interviewed lottery winners; many are broke in five years or less. Most say they wish they'd never won. There are some people who think they'll be happy if they find the right girl or the right guy.

Others wish to be taller or better looking, or to have a bigger chest or a smaller buttocks. "Yes" they say, "then I'll be happy."

I beg to differ.

I say the only way you can be truly happy is when you find a way to express who you really are. I mean, I can't change the fact that I'm barely 5-feet-4; but I can change my surroundings to make myself a better and happier guy. I can use whatever gifts I have and turn my life around. So can you.

Who are you?

What special gift do you have to offer to the world? Be honest with yourself. Please don't lie to me and the awaiting throng — those of us who need what you have to offer. Don't tell us you don't know what it is or that you can't do it because you're so busy. We want what you've got, but you won't give it to us. This little guy will tell you that, no matter how long you've sat on the outskirts watching everybody else have fun, now is the time for you to have a personal party of your own.

Maybe you like taking pictures. Maybe you've always wanted to give a speech to a frenzied crowd. Maybe you have a real love for kids and

Paint Your Picture for the World

you want to teach. Do it! Maybe you'll start off substituting. See how you like it, all the while keeping your present job. Let what's burning within you find its way out of you through expression. Maybe the thought of opening a flower shop gives you goosebumps. Maybe it's becoming a marine biologist that gets you excited. Who knows but you?

Have you ever seen a poor person who is as happy as a lark? Or a sick person who seems to be enjoying life more than you, a person who happens to be totally healthy? I'd be willing to bet these people have found a way to live life to the best of their ability, giving the world and their loved ones a taste of their God-given skills.

In Chapter Four, we talked about my shower experience. You've likely had a similar awakening. You, too, have dreamed of actually doing whatever you're dying to do, effortlessly. You've envisioned yourself so comfortable doing it that you could do it in front of hundreds, or even thousands of people. It may or may not be something that will make a ton of money for you. But when you picture yourself doing it, you feel as comfortable as a hot pig in cool slop. You inhale it, you roll in it, you eat it, and you drink it. I'm sure you're better looking than a pig, but you've got something in common with a pig psychologically, physically, and mentally: You wouldn't want to be in any other place.

I believe that whoever you are and whatever you look like, you've got an abundance of love for something deep down in your heart.

I'm not talking about making sure you're a great mom or being a great dad who provides for everyone. Those things are great, but I'm talking about doing something you love for *you*. The cliché is perhaps overused but does it ever apply here: "*You have to love yourself before you can love someone else.*"

FEELING TALL

The fastest way to the pathway of loving yourself is finding what makes you happy and doing it with passion and reckless abandon.

I'll never forget the story of Joe. I was a financial officer for a private school in New York. My office was located next to the principal's, and even though I wasn't supposed to be involved with curriculum and discipline, I often overheard the problems she faced.

My boss, Dr. Pearl Bell, was a great principal. She had one ability every principal should have: the ability to inspire terror. Even the toughest kids were reduced to babbling idiots when brought before her. One of her biggest problems was Joe. He wasn't really a bad kid, but he was always into mischief. You know the type — smart kid, but lacking in motivation and focus. He picked the wrong friends and was often the ringleader in foolishness. At 6-feet -3-inches tall, he was quite a character and always in front of the principal.

As Joe aprroached his senior year, it seemed everyone had given up on his becoming more than a high school graduate. Mrs. Bell wondered if he would even become that. But during Joe's senior year, Mrs. Bell hired a new art teacher. The teacher was organized and knew how to handle kids. She taught them how to express themselves in painting, poetry, and art.

The teacher was great. Quite by accident, Joe ended up in her class. At first, she too had a hard time with him. He got in trouble for smearing paint on kids and other art class "misdemeanors."

But after the first two weeks, he settled in. He was on time for class and attentive. His artwork over the grading period became beautiful. The art teacher said Joe he was the best student she had that year, and other students looked to him for leadership in the class.

One day, Mrs. Bell got the surprise of her life when Joe came into her office with tears in his eyes and a painting in his hand. It was a wonderful abstract. Joe looked at Mrs. Bell and, pointing to his painting, said, "Mrs. Bell, this is me, Joe." In other words, I was born to do this, this work represents who I am and what I'm all about.

Joe became an ideal student the rest of the year. His mother thanked us for saving him. It was all because he was able to get his God-given creative spirit out and tell the world about it. Life is too short to be in a situation you don't like. Again, I make no suggestion that you go to your boss and write "I quit" on his tie. But find a way at night or on the weekends to schedule some time to follow that star. You may have to get up an hour earlier every day to write or to study. Perhaps it will take night classes. Maybe you'll need to work part time or volunteer. But if you really want to score, you've got to *get in the game and play*.

I once read about a study that surveyed 1,000 people about happiness on the job. Sixty-two percent said they hated their jobs — they *hated* them! That's almost two-thirds. No wonder there is so much violence, poverty, and heartache in the world. And the real sadness is that if people could just find a way to move in the direction of fulfilling their life dreams, this kind of misery would almost be preventable. I don't want to be a part of that number at all; I want to be among the few who love life and everything about it.

You'll never really succeed at something unless you really like it. When I go out to speak or when I start to write, it's the most natural thing I do. In fact, I would do both for free. My family needs the check but I'd truly do both for nothing. I love spreading the message that you don't have to be unhappy with a situation you hate or people who bring you down when there is hope out there of doing other things or meeting other people who make you happy.

FEELING TALL

When I was in college, the big thing was to look and see what the "hot careers" were. My friends and I would read to see what we should major in to make sure we'd have a good job when we graduated. In fact, many college and business magazines still have articles on which jobs will be the most plentiful in the future. There are so many articles on the "hot jobs," but so few on finding the right career that will bring fulfillment and self-actualization.

I chose accounting as my major because the magazines said there would be a number of jobs available in 1985 in the field of financial services. Plus, my older brother Dave was a business administration major. So I signed on the line that said accounting. I realized after the first quarter that it wasn't all I thought it would be, and it took me eleven years to fully get out of it. That may sound sad, but better late than never.

Sadly enough, there are so many people out there who would love to squash your dream. When you realize what it is you really want to accomplish, even friends and family will poo-poo your vision. Don't let them. Don't allow them to bottle up what needs to be unleashed. Don't let them convince you to deny what you know to be true — that you have talent, you are special, and you have something to share with ordinary people like me.

I need what you've got. Indeed, the world needs what you've got. So in the words of Flip Wilson, the late 1970s variety show host and comic, *"Sock it to me, baby."*

CHAPTER EIGHT

Don't Let the Tall People Have All the Fun

Live Victoriously

You know what really makes me angry? When I see people who are so wounded by others that they fail to even try to do anything positive for themselves. They're reduced to living out the expectation of others. It's time, my friend, to have some fun.

Human nature is such that many people want to have fun but don't want you to have fun.

Don't let them get away with this attitude.

With more opportunity than ever out there, there's got to be some fun for you. When I think about my height, I sometimes think about the shortness of life. It is far too short. When the boy who slew Goliath, David, grew up and became king, he said this about life.

> "We spend our years as a tale that is told. The days of our years are threescore years and ten; and if by reason of strength they be fourscore years, yet is their strength labor and sorrow; for it is soon cut off, and we fly away."

FEELING TALL

Sounds pretty depressing, right? The fact is, we are all guaranteed a short life. Even if you live to be 100, in the grand scheme of things that's still relatively few years on this Earth. But a short life lived in unachieved goals and mediocrity is without question, sorrow. A life full of *life* is strength! It gives you a reason to go on every day and face the world with a smile.

It doesn't matter where you've been or what you are, you can start living your life today. It doesn't matter how you look or what your station is in life, you, too, can begin to have a life more abundant and captivating.

It can't happen overnight. But it can start right now. And you don't have to quit your day job to do it. Start with a few hours each week and begin living your dream and having fun.

I'm a big fan of national television news, and one of my favorite shows is *Larry King Live*. Recently, when news came out that King had signed a multimillion-dollar-per-year deal, he talked about his life. When the great interviewer was himself interviewed, he was asked what brought him his great success. King said he didn't work. "Excuse me?" the interviewer said. King said the has so much fun coming to work that he really doesn't consider it to be work. It's like going to play golf all day or shopping all day: You're just having fun. That's the point you have to get to. You have to get to the point where every day is fun. I love that word, *fun*.

Are you having fun?

If you aren't, then there is no better time to start than right now. Whether you're 16, 26, or 66, you need to have some fun. Aren't you sick of struggles every day? You should be. Get in the game and play ball with the big boys. Stop looking from the

Don't Let the Tall People Have All the Fun

sidelines. It's OK to cheer on others who have the courage to get out there and get involved, but I want *you* in the game too and I want you to be happy. The only way you'll find that happiness is to identify whatever it is you love, practice it until you get really good at it, and then get off your rear end and jump into the game.

Don't think for a moment that the people who are already playing are going to want to let you play. Most of them will think they're better, prettier, faster, and downright smarter than you. They've probably always underestimated you. But as the smart cookie you are, you've already done your homework.

You know the players and you're probably better at what they do than they are. You're ready for the game. Get in there and play. The people playing aren't better; they just believe in themselves.

Why should they have all the fun anyway?

Aren't you just as deserving? Open your mind and give yourself the chance to do something new and wonderful. You'll be amazed at how good you feel in the morning when you wake up and see the day as something new, exciting, and just for you. Just think: If you spend eight hours a day in a job you can't stand, imagine how productive you would be if those eight hours were spent doing something you truly loved. Here's what would happen: You'd have abundant energy to get things done and you'd do them so well you'd amaze yourself.

Since I've been in the business of journalism, both television and print, I've found that the most harsh critic of my work is me! I stress and obsess but I enjoy myself incredibly in the process. When I get involved in a news story, it doesn't feel like work. Sometimes I laugh because I can't believe they pay me to write and be on TV!

The pay isn't great, but the chance to do my "work" full time is awesome. I tell you, friend, once you start having fun, a new world opens to you that you would have never

FEELING TALL

imagined. You just need the confidence and the courage to get it done, *a little bit every day*.

I'd like to tell you about a friend I had named Robert. He was actually a friend I met through my wife. They were born on the same day and were great friends. I, too, have grown to love and respect him. But for years, he meandered from job to job looking for the thing that would fulfill him. He worked with troubled kids, one of the few jobs that he loved. He had a great personality, and from the outside he maintained a neat and clean persona. But as far as reaching his full potential was concerned, it just wasn't clicking. Robert, however, refused to give up.

I snickered a little when he tried to sell gold in a multilevel get-rich-quick scheme. He even convinced the superintendent of his building to let him run a fitness class out of the basement of the building. Then it was furniture. Robert got hooked up with a distributor and sold beds out of his home. My twelve-year-old still sleeps on one of the beds we bought from Robert. But the problem was that Robert had no car. So to make a delivery, he had to borrow transportation. Once promising a delivery of a mattress, he took it, with a boxspring, on the subway in New York City! He didn't care, he had made a promise he wasn't going to break.

Robert was the kind of guy who, no matter how badly you felt, would find a way to cheer you up. His smile and laughter were contagious, and when he was in the room he lit it up like no one I've ever met.

Then it happened one day.

Robert was asked to make a presentation on healthy living. He did it so well that others who listened invited him to do it elsewhere. He was a machine of facts, figures, and excellent statistics. Every time, he would blow his audience away with his smooth style.

He had found it! The thing that was not work but fun. Soon he joined a public speakers bureau and started making speeches all over the eastern part of the United States. I'd never seen him so happy. He was reaching his success in speaking just as I was reaching some success in television news. We often spoke about what it's like to finally arrive at a pinnacle of happiness. He was doing so well that he bought a Porsche. He was on top of the world.

Then triumph turned to sadness. I got a call from his sister Claudette. I could barely understand her words through the tears, but two words came through loud and clear. "Robert's dead!" On a winter night, he left his apartment in the Bronx headed for a speech he was to make in New Jersey. His car had hit a patch of ice; he'd lost control of it and crashed into a highway divider. The impact was so great that it killed him.

Robert's family still grieves his death, as do countless friends, including my wife and me.

But for some reason, I'm not totally sad when I think about him. I miss him, but whenever I think about him I think of a guy who refused to give up on his dream of happiness. I hate the tragic way he died, but I celebrate the fantastic way he lived.

Robert, you see, cared little about what others thought of his dreams. They were *his* dreams. Even he admitted later in his life that his past was questionable, but boy did he come back with a passion. At his funeral, an executive from his speaking company told the packed church that Robert was one of the organization's top producers. He was given the big jobs, the important speeches. The spokesman said Robert didn't understand the praise he consistently received. He was just out there doing his thing and having fun.

FEELING TALL

You may say Robert died tragically, but I say he lived victoriously. There are many people who go to their graves having never experienced true happiness. No one knows what tomorrow holds, so why wait to start finding out tomorrow? You must seize today.

Stop watching others have all the fun and have some fun yourself. Yes, it takes courage, yes, it takes guts, and yes, your friends and family may think you're crazy. But I guarantee you that when you get started, nothing will feel better than reaching those goals you set for yourself every day.

There is happiness out there to be had. Go out there and get some.